50 Sugar-Free Chocolate Dessert Recipes for Home

By: Kelly Johnson

Table of Contents

- Sugar-Free Chocolate Avocado Mousse
- Dark Chocolate Almond Bark with Sea Salt
- Sugar-Free Chocolate Truffles with Coconut
- Flourless Sugar-Free Chocolate Cake
- Sugar-Free Chocolate Chia Pudding
- Sugar-Free Chocolate Peanut Butter Cups
- Keto Chocolate Cheesecake Brownies
- Sugar-Free Chocolate Banana Bread
- Sugar-Free Chocolate Zucchini Muffins
- Sugar-Free Chocolate Protein Balls
- Sugar-Free Chocolate Coconut Macaroons
- Sugar-Free Chocolate Covered Strawberries
- Sugar-Free Chocolate Chip Cookies with Almonds
- Sugar-Free Chocolate Hazelnut Spread
- Sugar-Free Chocolate Pudding Pie with Almond Crust
- Sugar-Free Chocolate Almond Butter Fudge
- Sugar-Free Chocolate Raspberry Trifle
- Sugar-Free Chocolate Mint Ice Cream
- Sugar-Free Chocolate Pecan Pie Bars
- Sugar-Free Chocolate Espresso Brownies
- Sugar-Free Chocolate Coconut Bliss Balls
- Sugar-Free Chocolate Pumpkin Spice Cupcakes
- Sugar-Free Chocolate Avocado Brownies
- Sugar-Free Chocolate Protein Smoothie Bowl
- Sugar-Free Chocolate Almond Biscotti
- Sugar-Free Chocolate Cherry Cheesecake Bites
- Sugar-Free Chocolate Peanut Butter Protein Bars
- Sugar-Free Chocolate Oatmeal Cookies
- Sugar-Free Chocolate Chia Seed Pudding Parfait
- Sugar-Free Chocolate Hazelnut Torte
- Sugar-Free Chocolate Coconut Flour Pancakes
- Sugar-Free Chocolate Cashew Cheesecake
- Sugar-Free Chocolate Banana Ice Cream
- Sugar-Free Chocolate Almond Joy Bites
- Sugar-Free Chocolate Raspberry Coconut Bars

- Sugar-Free Chocolate Pecan Pralines
- Sugar-Free Chocolate Chia Seed Energy Balls
- Sugar-Free Chocolate Coconut Flour Brownies
- Sugar-Free Chocolate Peanut Butter Energy Bites
- Sugar-Free Chocolate Cherry Smoothie
- Sugar-Free Chocolate Coconut Cream Pie
- Sugar-Free Chocolate Macadamia Nut Cookies
- Sugar-Free Chocolate Pistachio Truffles
- Sugar-Free Chocolate Raspberry Cake Roll
- Sugar-Free Chocolate Orange Cheesecake
- Sugar-Free Chocolate Walnut Blondies
- Sugar-Free Chocolate Peanut Butter Nice Cream
- Sugar-Free Chocolate Avocado Cookies
- Sugar-Free Chocolate Hazelnut Granola Bars
- Sugar-Free Chocolate Raspberry Chia Popsicles

Sugar-Free Chocolate Avocado Mousse

Ingredients:

- 2 ripe avocados
- 1/4 cup unsweetened cocoa powder
- 1/4 cup unsweetened almond milk (or any milk of your choice)
- 1 teaspoon vanilla extract
- 2-3 tablespoons maple syrup or honey (optional, for added sweetness)
- Pinch of salt
- Fresh berries, for garnish (optional)
- Shredded coconut or chopped nuts, for garnish (optional)

Instructions:

1. Cut the avocados in half and remove the pits. Scoop the flesh into a blender or food processor.
2. Add the unsweetened cocoa powder, unsweetened almond milk, vanilla extract, maple syrup or honey (if using), and a pinch of salt to the blender or food processor.
3. Blend the ingredients until smooth and creamy, scraping down the sides of the blender or food processor as needed to ensure everything is well combined.
4. Taste the mousse and adjust the sweetness as desired by adding more maple syrup or honey, if needed.
5. Once the mousse reaches your desired consistency and sweetness, transfer it to serving dishes or small bowls.
6. Cover the mousse with plastic wrap and refrigerate for at least 30 minutes to chill and allow the flavors to meld together.
7. Before serving, garnish the Sugar-Free Chocolate Avocado Mousse with fresh berries, shredded coconut, chopped nuts, or any other toppings of your choice.
8. Enjoy your delicious and healthy dessert guilt-free!

This Sugar-Free Chocolate Avocado Mousse is perfect for satisfying your chocolate cravings without the added sugar. Plus, it's packed with nutrients from the avocado and cocoa powder, making it a wholesome treat for any occasion.

Dark Chocolate Almond Bark with Sea Salt

Ingredients:

- 10 ounces (about 280g) dark chocolate (at least 70% cocoa), chopped
- 1 cup whole almonds, toasted
- Coarse sea salt, for sprinkling

Instructions:

1. Line a baking sheet with parchment paper or a silicone baking mat.
2. In a microwave-safe bowl, melt the chopped dark chocolate in 30-second intervals, stirring well after each interval, until smooth and fully melted. Alternatively, you can melt the chocolate using a double boiler on the stove.
3. Once the chocolate is melted, stir in the toasted whole almonds until they are evenly coated with chocolate.
4. Pour the chocolate-coated almonds onto the prepared baking sheet, spreading them out into an even layer with a spatula.
5. Sprinkle coarse sea salt evenly over the top of the chocolate-coated almonds.
6. Place the baking sheet in the refrigerator for about 30 minutes, or until the chocolate has set completely.
7. Once the chocolate has hardened, break the Dark Chocolate Almond Bark into bite-sized pieces using your hands or a knife.
8. Transfer the almond bark pieces to an airtight container or package them in decorative bags or boxes for gifting.
9. Enjoy your delicious Dark Chocolate Almond Bark with Sea Salt as a snack or dessert!

This indulgent treat is perfect for satisfying your sweet cravings while also providing a satisfying crunch and a hint of saltiness from the sea salt. It's also a wonderful homemade gift for friends and family during the holiday season or any special occasion.

Sugar-Free Chocolate Truffles with Coconut

Ingredients:

- 8 ounces (about 225g) dark chocolate (at least 70% cocoa), chopped
- 1/2 cup canned coconut milk (full-fat)
- 1 teaspoon vanilla extract
- Unsweetened shredded coconut, for coating

Instructions:

1. In a small saucepan, heat the coconut milk over medium heat until it starts to simmer. Remove the saucepan from the heat.
2. Place the chopped dark chocolate in a heatproof bowl. Pour the hot coconut milk over the chocolate and let it sit for 1-2 minutes to soften the chocolate.
3. Gently whisk the chocolate and coconut milk together until smooth and well combined. If needed, you can return the bowl to a double boiler or microwave in short intervals to melt any remaining chocolate pieces.
4. Stir in the vanilla extract until incorporated.
5. Cover the bowl with plastic wrap and refrigerate the chocolate mixture for at least 2 hours, or until firm.
6. Once the chocolate mixture has chilled and hardened, use a spoon or melon baller to scoop out small portions and roll them into balls between your palms.
7. Roll the chocolate truffles in unsweetened shredded coconut until they are evenly coated.
8. Place the coated truffles on a baking sheet lined with parchment paper and return them to the refrigerator to set for another 30 minutes.
9. Once set, transfer the Sugar-Free Chocolate Truffles with Coconut to an airtight container and store them in the refrigerator until ready to serve.
10. Enjoy your delicious and guilt-free chocolate truffles as a satisfying snack or dessert!

These Sugar-Free Chocolate Truffles with Coconut are perfect for satisfying your sweet tooth without the added sugar. Plus, they're dairy-free and vegan-friendly, making them suitable for a variety of dietary preferences.

Flourless Sugar-Free Chocolate Cake

Ingredients:

- 8 ounces (about 225g) dark chocolate (at least 70% cocoa), chopped
- 1/2 cup unsalted butter, cubed
- 1/4 cup unsweetened cocoa powder
- 4 large eggs, separated
- 1/2 cup granulated erythritol or monk fruit sweetener
- 1 teaspoon vanilla extract
- Pinch of salt
- Whipped cream or berries, for serving (optional)

Instructions:

1. Preheat your oven to 350°F (175°C). Grease a 9-inch round cake pan and line the bottom with parchment paper.
2. In a heatproof bowl set over a pot of simmering water (double boiler), melt the chopped dark chocolate and cubed unsalted butter together, stirring occasionally, until smooth and fully melted.
3. Remove the bowl from the heat and whisk in the unsweetened cocoa powder until well combined. Let the mixture cool slightly.
4. In a separate bowl, beat the egg yolks with the granulated erythritol or monk fruit sweetener and vanilla extract until pale and creamy.
5. Gradually add the melted chocolate mixture to the beaten egg yolks, whisking continuously until smooth and well combined.
6. In another clean bowl, beat the egg whites with a pinch of salt until stiff peaks form.
7. Gently fold the beaten egg whites into the chocolate mixture until no white streaks remain, being careful not to deflate the egg whites.
8. Pour the batter into the prepared cake pan and smooth the top with a spatula.
9. Bake the flourless chocolate cake in the preheated oven for 25-30 minutes, or until the top is set and a toothpick inserted into the center comes out with a few moist crumbs.
10. Remove the cake from the oven and let it cool in the pan for 10 minutes before transferring it to a wire rack to cool completely.
11. Once cooled, slice the Flourless Sugar-Free Chocolate Cake into wedges and serve with whipped cream or berries, if desired.
12. Enjoy your delicious and guilt-free chocolate cake!

This Flourless Sugar-Free Chocolate Cake is rich, fudgy, and packed with chocolate flavor, making it the perfect dessert for special occasions or any time you're craving something sweet and satisfying.

Sugar-Free Chocolate Chia Pudding

Ingredients:

- 1/4 cup chia seeds
- 1 cup unsweetened almond milk (or any milk of your choice)
- 2 tablespoons unsweetened cocoa powder
- 1-2 tablespoons granulated erythritol or monk fruit sweetener, to taste
- 1/2 teaspoon vanilla extract
- Pinch of salt
- Optional toppings: fresh berries, sliced bananas, chopped nuts, shredded coconut

Instructions:

1. In a mixing bowl, combine the chia seeds, unsweetened almond milk, unsweetened cocoa powder, granulated erythritol or monk fruit sweetener, vanilla extract, and a pinch of salt. Stir well to combine.
2. Cover the bowl and refrigerate the chocolate chia pudding mixture for at least 2 hours, or overnight, to allow the chia seeds to absorb the liquid and thicken.
3. After the pudding has set, give it a good stir to redistribute the chia seeds evenly.
4. Divide the chocolate chia pudding into individual serving cups or jars.
5. Serve the Sugar-Free Chocolate Chia Pudding cold, topped with your favorite toppings such as fresh berries, sliced bananas, chopped nuts, or shredded coconut.
6. Enjoy your delicious and guilt-free chocolate chia pudding as a satisfying dessert or snack!

This Sugar-Free Chocolate Chia Pudding is not only tasty but also nutritious, making it a perfect choice for a quick and easy breakfast, snack, or dessert. Plus, it's vegan, gluten-free, and low-carb, making it suitable for a variety of dietary preferences.

Sugar-Free Chocolate Peanut Butter Cups

Ingredients:

For the chocolate coating:

- 6 ounces (about 170g) sugar-free dark chocolate, chopped
- 1 tablespoon coconut oil

For the peanut butter filling:

- 1/2 cup unsweetened creamy peanut butter
- 2 tablespoons powdered erythritol or monk fruit sweetener
- 1/2 teaspoon vanilla extract
- Pinch of salt

Instructions:

1. Line a muffin tin with paper or silicone cupcake liners and set it aside.
2. In a microwave-safe bowl, combine the chopped sugar-free dark chocolate and coconut oil. Microwave in 30-second intervals, stirring well after each interval, until the chocolate is fully melted and smooth.
3. Spoon a small amount of the melted chocolate into the bottom of each cupcake liner, spreading it evenly to coat the bottom and slightly up the sides. Place the muffin tin in the refrigerator to allow the chocolate to set while you prepare the peanut butter filling.
4. In a mixing bowl, combine the unsweetened creamy peanut butter, powdered erythritol or monk fruit sweetener, vanilla extract, and a pinch of salt. Stir until smooth and well combined.
5. Remove the muffin tin from the refrigerator and spoon a small amount of the peanut butter filling on top of the set chocolate layer in each cupcake liner, spreading it out evenly.
6. Spoon the remaining melted chocolate over the peanut butter filling in each cupcake liner, covering it completely and smoothing the top with a spoon.
7. Return the muffin tin to the refrigerator and chill the sugar-free chocolate peanut butter cups for at least 1 hour, or until firm and set.
8. Once set, remove the chocolate peanut butter cups from the muffin tin and store them in an airtight container in the refrigerator until ready to serve.
9. Enjoy your delicious and guilt-free Sugar-Free Chocolate Peanut Butter Cups as a satisfying snack or dessert!

These homemade chocolate peanut butter cups are perfect for satisfying your sweet cravings without the added sugar. Plus, they're easy to make and customizable to suit your taste preferences.

Keto Chocolate Cheesecake Brownies

Ingredients:

For the brownie layer:

- 1/2 cup unsalted butter
- 3/4 cup sugar-free dark chocolate chips
- 1/2 cup granulated erythritol or monk fruit sweetener
- 2 large eggs
- 1 teaspoon vanilla extract
- 1/2 cup almond flour
- 2 tablespoons unsweetened cocoa powder
- 1/4 teaspoon salt

For the cheesecake layer:

- 8 ounces cream cheese, softened
- 1/4 cup granulated erythritol or monk fruit sweetener
- 1 large egg
- 1/2 teaspoon vanilla extract

Instructions:

1. Preheat your oven to 350°F (175°C). Grease an 8x8-inch baking dish or line it with parchment paper, leaving some overhang for easy removal.
2. In a microwave-safe bowl, melt the unsalted butter and sugar-free dark chocolate chips together in 30-second intervals, stirring well after each interval, until smooth and fully melted.
3. In a separate mixing bowl, whisk together the granulated erythritol or monk fruit sweetener, eggs, and vanilla extract until smooth.
4. Gradually pour the melted chocolate mixture into the egg mixture, whisking continuously until well combined.
5. Stir in the almond flour, unsweetened cocoa powder, and salt until just combined. Be careful not to overmix.
6. Pour the brownie batter into the prepared baking dish and spread it out evenly with a spatula.
7. In another mixing bowl, beat the softened cream cheese, granulated erythritol or monk fruit sweetener, egg, and vanilla extract together until smooth and creamy.
8. Spoon dollops of the cheesecake mixture over the brownie batter in the baking dish.

9. Use a knife or skewer to swirl the cheesecake mixture into the brownie batter, creating a marbled effect.
10. Bake the Keto Chocolate Cheesecake Brownies in the preheated oven for 25-30 minutes, or until the edges are set and the center is slightly jiggly.
11. Remove the baking dish from the oven and let the brownies cool completely in the pan on a wire rack.
12. Once cooled, refrigerate the brownies for at least 2 hours, or until firm and set.
13. Slice the chilled brownies into squares and serve.
14. Enjoy your delicious and indulgent Keto Chocolate Cheesecake Brownies as a satisfying low-carb dessert!

These Keto Chocolate Cheesecake Brownies are perfect for satisfying your sweet cravings while still adhering to your ketogenic lifestyle. They're rich, creamy, and packed with chocolatey goodness, making them a favorite among keto and non-keto eaters alike.

Sugar-Free Chocolate Banana Bread

Ingredients:

- 2 ripe bananas, mashed
- 2 large eggs
- 1/4 cup unsweetened applesauce
- 1/4 cup coconut oil, melted
- 1 teaspoon vanilla extract
- 1 cup almond flour
- 1/4 cup unsweetened cocoa powder
- 1 teaspoon baking powder
- 1/2 teaspoon baking soda
- Pinch of salt
- Optional add-ins: chopped nuts, sugar-free chocolate chips

Instructions:

1. Preheat your oven to 350°F (175°C). Grease a 9x5-inch loaf pan or line it with parchment paper.
2. In a large mixing bowl, mash the ripe bananas with a fork until smooth.
3. Add the eggs, unsweetened applesauce, melted coconut oil, and vanilla extract to the mashed bananas. Whisk together until well combined.
4. In a separate mixing bowl, whisk together the almond flour, unsweetened cocoa powder, baking powder, baking soda, and a pinch of salt.
5. Gradually add the dry ingredients to the wet ingredients, stirring until just combined. Be careful not to overmix.
6. If desired, fold in any optional add-ins such as chopped nuts or sugar-free chocolate chips.
7. Pour the batter into the prepared loaf pan and spread it out evenly with a spatula.
8. Bake the Sugar-Free Chocolate Banana Bread in the preheated oven for 40-45 minutes, or until a toothpick inserted into the center comes out clean.
9. Remove the loaf pan from the oven and let the banana bread cool in the pan for 10-15 minutes before transferring it to a wire rack to cool completely.
10. Once cooled, slice the Sugar-Free Chocolate Banana Bread into thick slices and serve.
11. Enjoy your delicious and healthier Sugar-Free Chocolate Banana Bread as a satisfying snack or breakfast treat!

This Sugar-Free Chocolate Banana Bread is moist, flavorful, and perfect for using up ripe bananas without the need for added sugar. It's a great option for those following a low-sugar or diabetic-friendly diet, and it's sure to become a family favorite!

Sugar-Free Chocolate Zucchini Muffins

Ingredients:

- 1 cup grated zucchini (about 1 medium zucchini)
- 2 large eggs
- 1/4 cup unsweetened applesauce
- 1/4 cup coconut oil, melted
- 1 teaspoon vanilla extract
- 1/2 cup granulated erythritol or monk fruit sweetener
- 1 cup almond flour
- 1/4 cup unsweetened cocoa powder
- 1 teaspoon baking powder
- 1/2 teaspoon baking soda
- Pinch of salt
- Optional add-ins: sugar-free chocolate chips, chopped nuts

Instructions:

1. Preheat your oven to 350°F (175°C). Grease a muffin tin or line it with paper liners.
2. In a mixing bowl, combine the grated zucchini, eggs, unsweetened applesauce, melted coconut oil, vanilla extract, and granulated erythritol or monk fruit sweetener. Mix well until thoroughly combined.
3. In a separate mixing bowl, whisk together the almond flour, unsweetened cocoa powder, baking powder, baking soda, and a pinch of salt.
4. Gradually add the dry ingredients to the wet ingredients, stirring until just combined. Be careful not to overmix.
5. If desired, fold in any optional add-ins such as sugar-free chocolate chips or chopped nuts.
6. Spoon the batter into the prepared muffin tin, filling each muffin cup about 3/4 full.
7. Bake the Sugar-Free Chocolate Zucchini Muffins in the preheated oven for 18-20 minutes, or until a toothpick inserted into the center comes out clean.
8. Remove the muffin tin from the oven and let the muffins cool in the tin for 5 minutes before transferring them to a wire rack to cool completely.
9. Once cooled, serve the Sugar-Free Chocolate Zucchini Muffins and enjoy as a delicious and nutritious snack or breakfast treat!

These muffins are moist, chocolaty, and packed with fiber and nutrients from the zucchini. They're perfect for those looking to satisfy their sweet tooth without the added sugar, and they're sure to become a favorite in your household!

Sugar-Free Chocolate Protein Balls

Ingredients:

- 1 cup rolled oats
- 1/2 cup unsweetened shredded coconut
- 1/4 cup unsweetened cocoa powder
- 1/2 cup natural peanut butter or almond butter
- 1/4 cup sugar-free maple syrup or honey alternative
- 1 scoop chocolate protein powder
- 1 teaspoon vanilla extract
- Pinch of salt
- Optional add-ins: sugar-free chocolate chips, chopped nuts, chia seeds

Instructions:

1. In a food processor, combine the rolled oats, unsweetened shredded coconut, unsweetened cocoa powder, natural peanut butter or almond butter, sugar-free maple syrup or honey alternative, chocolate protein powder, vanilla extract, and a pinch of salt.
2. Pulse the ingredients until well combined and the mixture starts to come together. If the mixture seems too dry, you can add a little more peanut butter or almond butter. If it's too wet, add more oats or protein powder.
3. If desired, fold in any optional add-ins such as sugar-free chocolate chips, chopped nuts, or chia seeds.
4. Once the mixture has reached a dough-like consistency, use your hands to roll it into bite-sized balls.
5. Place the Sugar-Free Chocolate Protein Balls on a baking sheet lined with parchment paper and refrigerate them for at least 30 minutes to firm up.
6. Once firm, transfer the protein balls to an airtight container and store them in the refrigerator until ready to eat.
7. Enjoy your delicious and nutritious Sugar-Free Chocolate Protein Balls as a pre-workout snack, post-workout refuel, or anytime you need a healthy pick-me-up!

These protein balls are packed with fiber, protein, and healthy fats, making them a perfect snack to keep you energized and satisfied throughout the day. Plus, they're customizable to suit your taste preferences, so feel free to get creative with your add-ins!

Sugar-Free Chocolate Coconut Macaroons

Ingredients:

- 2 cups unsweetened shredded coconut
- 1/3 cup unsweetened cocoa powder
- 1/2 cup granulated erythritol or monk fruit sweetener
- 3 large egg whites
- 1 teaspoon vanilla extract
- Pinch of salt
- Optional: sugar-free chocolate chips

Instructions:

1. Preheat your oven to 325°F (160°C). Line a baking sheet with parchment paper or a silicone baking mat.
2. In a large mixing bowl, combine the unsweetened shredded coconut, unsweetened cocoa powder, and granulated erythritol or monk fruit sweetener. Stir until well combined.
3. In a separate mixing bowl, beat the egg whites with a pinch of salt until stiff peaks form.
4. Gently fold the beaten egg whites into the coconut mixture until evenly combined. Be careful not to deflate the egg whites too much.
5. Stir in the vanilla extract until incorporated. If desired, fold in some sugar-free chocolate chips for extra flavor.
6. Using a spoon or cookie scoop, drop rounded tablespoons of the coconut mixture onto the prepared baking sheet, spacing them about 1 inch apart.
7. Bake the Sugar-Free Chocolate Coconut Macaroons in the preheated oven for 15-18 minutes, or until the edges are golden brown and the tops are set.
8. Remove the baking sheet from the oven and let the macaroons cool on the pan for 5 minutes before transferring them to a wire rack to cool completely.
9. Once cooled, store the Sugar-Free Chocolate Coconut Macaroons in an airtight container at room temperature for up to 5 days, or in the refrigerator for longer shelf life.
10. Enjoy your delicious and guilt-free Sugar-Free Chocolate Coconut Macaroons as a satisfying snack or dessert!

These macaroons are chewy, chocolaty, and perfect for anyone looking to satisfy their sweet tooth without the added sugar. Plus, they're gluten-free and dairy-free, making them suitable for a variety of dietary preferences.

Sugar-Free Chocolate Covered Strawberries

Ingredients:

- Fresh strawberries, rinsed and dried
- 4 ounces (about 113g) sugar-free dark chocolate, chopped
- 1 tablespoon coconut oil
- Optional toppings: chopped nuts, shredded coconut, sea salt

Instructions:

1. Line a baking sheet with parchment paper or a silicone baking mat.
2. In a microwave-safe bowl, combine the chopped sugar-free dark chocolate and coconut oil. Microwave in 30-second intervals, stirring well after each interval, until the chocolate is fully melted and smooth.
3. Holding a strawberry by the stem, dip it into the melted chocolate, swirling it around to coat it evenly.
4. Lift the chocolate-coated strawberry out of the bowl and allow any excess chocolate to drip off.
5. Place the chocolate-covered strawberry on the prepared baking sheet.
6. If desired, sprinkle the top of the chocolate-covered strawberry with your choice of toppings, such as chopped nuts, shredded coconut, or a sprinkle of sea salt.
7. Repeat the dipping process with the remaining strawberries until they are all coated in chocolate.
8. Once all the strawberries are coated, place the baking sheet in the refrigerator for about 15-20 minutes, or until the chocolate has set.
9. Once set, remove the Sugar-Free Chocolate Covered Strawberries from the refrigerator and serve immediately, or store them in an airtight container in the refrigerator until ready to enjoy.
10. Enjoy your delicious and guilt-free Sugar-Free Chocolate Covered Strawberries as a delightful dessert or snack!

These chocolate-covered strawberries are a perfect way to satisfy your sweet cravings without the added sugar. Plus, they're packed with antioxidants from the dark chocolate and vitamin C from the strawberries, making them a healthier option for indulging in a sweet treat.

Sugar-Free Chocolate Chip Cookies with Almonds

Ingredients:

- 1 cup almond flour
- 1/4 cup granulated erythritol or monk fruit sweetener
- 1/4 teaspoon baking soda
- Pinch of salt
- 1/4 cup unsalted butter, melted
- 1 large egg
- 1 teaspoon vanilla extract
- 1/4 cup sugar-free chocolate chips
- 1/4 cup chopped almonds

Instructions:

1. Preheat your oven to 350°F (175°C). Line a baking sheet with parchment paper or a silicone baking mat.
2. In a mixing bowl, whisk together the almond flour, granulated erythritol or monk fruit sweetener, baking soda, and a pinch of salt until well combined.
3. In a separate mixing bowl, whisk together the melted unsalted butter, egg, and vanilla extract until smooth.
4. Gradually add the wet ingredients to the dry ingredients, stirring until a dough forms.
5. Fold in the sugar-free chocolate chips and chopped almonds until evenly distributed throughout the dough.
6. Using a spoon or cookie scoop, drop rounded tablespoons of dough onto the prepared baking sheet, spacing them about 2 inches apart.
7. Use your fingers or the back of a spoon to gently flatten each cookie slightly.
8. Bake the Sugar-Free Chocolate Chip Cookies with Almonds in the preheated oven for 10-12 minutes, or until the edges are golden brown.
9. Remove the baking sheet from the oven and let the cookies cool on the pan for 5 minutes before transferring them to a wire rack to cool completely.
10. Once cooled, serve the Sugar-Free Chocolate Chip Cookies with Almonds and enjoy as a delicious and guilt-free snack or dessert!

These cookies are perfect for anyone looking to satisfy their sweet tooth without the added sugar. Plus, they're packed with protein and healthy fats from the almonds and almond flour, making them a healthier alternative to traditional chocolate chip cookies.

Sugar-Free Chocolate Hazelnut Spread

Ingredients:

- 1 cup hazelnuts
- 1/4 cup unsweetened cocoa powder
- 1/4 cup powdered erythritol or monk fruit sweetener
- 1 tablespoon coconut oil
- 1 teaspoon vanilla extract
- Pinch of salt

Instructions:

1. Preheat your oven to 350°F (175°C). Spread the hazelnuts in a single layer on a baking sheet and roast them in the preheated oven for 10-12 minutes, or until fragrant and lightly golden brown. Keep an eye on them to prevent burning.
2. Once roasted, remove the hazelnuts from the oven and let them cool slightly. Rub the hazelnuts between your hands or in a clean kitchen towel to remove the skins. It's okay if some skin remains.
3. Transfer the peeled hazelnuts to a food processor and process them until they form a smooth and creamy nut butter consistency, scraping down the sides of the bowl as needed. This process can take several minutes depending on your food processor.
4. Add the unsweetened cocoa powder, powdered erythritol or monk fruit sweetener, coconut oil, vanilla extract, and a pinch of salt to the food processor with the hazelnut butter.
5. Process the mixture again until all the ingredients are well combined and the spread is smooth and creamy.
6. Taste the Sugar-Free Chocolate Hazelnut Spread and adjust the sweetness or cocoa flavor to your liking by adding more sweetener or cocoa powder if needed.
7. Once satisfied with the taste and consistency, transfer the chocolate hazelnut spread to a clean jar or airtight container for storage.
8. Store the Sugar-Free Chocolate Hazelnut Spread in the refrigerator for up to two weeks.
9. Enjoy your delicious and guilt-free spread on toast, pancakes, waffles, fruit, or use it in recipes as a substitute for Nutella or other chocolate spreads!

This homemade Sugar-Free Chocolate Hazelnut Spread is perfect for anyone looking to enjoy the rich flavor of chocolate and hazelnuts without the added sugar. Plus, it's easy to make and customizable to suit your taste preferences.

Sugar-Free Chocolate Pudding Pie with Almond Crust

Ingredients:

For the almond crust:

- 1 1/2 cups almond flour
- 1/4 cup granulated erythritol or monk fruit sweetener
- 1/4 cup unsalted butter, melted
- 1/2 teaspoon vanilla extract
- Pinch of salt

For the sugar-free chocolate pudding filling:

- 2 1/2 cups unsweetened almond milk (or any milk of your choice)
- 1/4 cup unsweetened cocoa powder
- 1/4 cup cornstarch
- 1/4 cup granulated erythritol or monk fruit sweetener
- 1 teaspoon vanilla extract
- Pinch of salt

Instructions:

1. Preheat your oven to 350°F (175°C). Grease a 9-inch pie dish or tart pan.
2. In a mixing bowl, combine the almond flour, granulated erythritol or monk fruit sweetener, melted unsalted butter, vanilla extract, and a pinch of salt. Stir until well combined and the mixture resembles coarse crumbs.
3. Press the almond mixture into the bottom and up the sides of the prepared pie dish or tart pan to form the crust.
4. Bake the almond crust in the preheated oven for 10-12 minutes, or until lightly golden brown. Remove from the oven and let it cool completely.
5. While the crust is cooling, prepare the sugar-free chocolate pudding filling. In a saucepan, whisk together the unsweetened almond milk, unsweetened cocoa powder, cornstarch, granulated erythritol or monk fruit sweetener, vanilla extract, and a pinch of salt.
6. Place the saucepan over medium heat and cook the mixture, stirring constantly, until it thickens and comes to a gentle boil.
7. Once the pudding mixture has thickened, remove it from the heat and let it cool slightly.
8. Pour the chocolate pudding filling into the cooled almond crust, spreading it out evenly with a spatula.

9. Place the pie in the refrigerator to chill for at least 2 hours, or until the pudding is set.
10. Once set, slice the Sugar-Free Chocolate Pudding Pie with Almond Crust into wedges and serve.
11. Enjoy your delicious and guilt-free dessert as a satisfying treat!

This Sugar-Free Chocolate Pudding Pie with Almond Crust is perfect for anyone looking to indulge in a sweet dessert without the added sugar. Plus, the nutty almond crust adds a delicious flavor and texture to the creamy chocolate pudding filling.

Sugar-Free Chocolate Almond Butter Fudge

Ingredients:

- 1 cup almond butter
- 1/2 cup coconut oil
- 1/4 cup unsweetened cocoa powder
- 1/4 cup powdered erythritol or your preferred sugar-free sweetener
- 1 teaspoon vanilla extract
- A pinch of salt
- Optional toppings: chopped almonds, shredded coconut, or sugar-free chocolate chips

Instructions:

1. In a microwave-safe bowl or on the stovetop, melt the almond butter and coconut oil together until smooth. If using a microwave, heat in 30-second intervals, stirring in between until fully melted.
2. Once melted, stir in the cocoa powder, powdered erythritol, vanilla extract, and a pinch of salt until well combined and smooth. Taste and adjust sweetness if needed by adding more sweetener.
3. Line a small baking dish or container with parchment paper, leaving some overhang for easy removal later.
4. Pour the fudge mixture into the prepared dish and spread it out evenly.
5. If desired, sprinkle optional toppings like chopped almonds, shredded coconut, or sugar-free chocolate chips over the top of the fudge.
6. Place the dish in the refrigerator and chill for at least 2 hours, or until the fudge is firm.
7. Once set, lift the fudge out of the dish using the parchment paper overhang and cut it into squares or bars.
8. Store the fudge in an airtight container in the refrigerator for up to two weeks. Enjoy your sugar-free chocolate almond butter fudge as a delicious and guilt-free treat!

Sugar-Free Chocolate Raspberry Trifle

Ingredients:

For the Chocolate Cake:

- 1 1/2 cups almond flour
- 1/4 cup unsweetened cocoa powder
- 1/4 cup powdered erythritol or your preferred sugar-free sweetener
- 1/2 teaspoon baking soda
- 1/4 teaspoon salt
- 3 large eggs
- 1/4 cup coconut oil, melted
- 1/4 cup unsweetened almond milk
- 1 teaspoon vanilla extract

For the Trifle Layers:

- 2 cups sugar-free whipped cream or whipped coconut cream
- 2 cups fresh raspberries
- Sugar-free chocolate shavings or cocoa powder for garnish

Instructions:

For the Chocolate Cake:

1. Preheat your oven to 350°F (175°C). Grease a small baking dish or cake pan with coconut oil or line it with parchment paper.
2. In a mixing bowl, whisk together the almond flour, cocoa powder, powdered erythritol, baking soda, and salt until well combined.
3. In another bowl, beat the eggs, melted coconut oil, almond milk, and vanilla extract together until smooth.
4. Gradually add the dry ingredients to the wet ingredients, stirring until a smooth batter forms.
5. Pour the batter into the prepared baking dish and spread it out evenly.
6. Bake in the preheated oven for 20-25 minutes, or until a toothpick inserted into the center comes out clean.
7. Allow the cake to cool completely before assembling the trifle.

Assembling the Trifle:

1. Once the cake has cooled, cut it into small cubes.
2. In a trifle dish or individual serving glasses, start by layering half of the chocolate cake cubes at the bottom.
3. Spread a layer of sugar-free whipped cream or whipped coconut cream over the cake cubes.
4. Add a layer of fresh raspberries on top of the cream layer.
5. Repeat the layers with the remaining cake cubes, whipped cream, and raspberries.
6. Finish off the trifle with a final layer of whipped cream on top.
7. Garnish with sugar-free chocolate shavings or a sprinkle of cocoa powder.
8. Refrigerate the trifle for at least 1 hour before serving to allow the flavors to meld together.
9. Serve chilled and enjoy your sugar-free chocolate raspberry trifle!

This dessert is perfect for special occasions or any time you're craving a sweet treat without the added sugar.

Sugar-Free Chocolate Mint Ice Cream

Ingredients:

- 2 cans (14 oz each) full-fat coconut milk, chilled in the refrigerator overnight
- 1/2 cup unsweetened cocoa powder
- 1/2 cup powdered erythritol or your preferred sugar-free sweetener
- 1 teaspoon vanilla extract
- 1/2 teaspoon peppermint extract
- A pinch of salt
- Optional: sugar-free chocolate chips or chopped dark chocolate

Instructions:

1. Chill Equipment: Place a large mixing bowl and the bowl of your ice cream maker in the freezer for about 10-15 minutes to chill.
2. Prepare Coconut Milk: Open the cans of chilled coconut milk and scoop out the solid coconut cream that has risen to the top, leaving behind the liquid. Transfer the coconut cream to the chilled mixing bowl.
3. Mix Ingredients: Add cocoa powder, powdered erythritol, vanilla extract, peppermint extract, and a pinch of salt to the coconut cream.
4. Beat Ingredients: Using a hand mixer or stand mixer, beat the ingredients together until well combined and smooth. You can also use a whisk if you don't have a mixer, but it will take a bit longer.
5. Taste and Adjust: Taste the mixture and adjust sweetness or mint flavor according to your preference.
6. Chill Mixture: Cover the bowl with plastic wrap or a lid and refrigerate the mixture for at least 1-2 hours, or until thoroughly chilled.
7. Churn Ice Cream: Once the mixture is chilled, pour it into your ice cream maker and churn according to the manufacturer's instructions until it reaches a soft-serve consistency.
8. Add Chocolate: If desired, add sugar-free chocolate chips or chopped dark chocolate during the last few minutes of churning.
9. Transfer and Freeze: Transfer the churned ice cream to a freezer-safe container, smoothing the top with a spatula. Cover tightly with a lid or plastic wrap and freeze for at least 4 hours, or until firm.
10. Serve: Allow the ice cream to sit at room temperature for a few minutes before scooping and serving. Enjoy your sugar-free chocolate mint ice cream on its own or with a drizzle of sugar-free chocolate sauce or whipped cream!

This ice cream is creamy, rich, and packed with refreshing mint flavor, making it a perfect treat for hot summer days or any time you're craving a cool dessert.

Sugar-Free Chocolate Pecan Pie Bars

Ingredients:

For the Crust:

- 1 cup almond flour
- 1/4 cup coconut flour
- 1/4 cup powdered erythritol or your preferred sugar-free sweetener
- 1/4 teaspoon salt
- 1/4 cup coconut oil, melted
- 1 large egg

For the Filling:

- 1 cup chopped pecans
- 1/2 cup powdered erythritol or your preferred sugar-free sweetener
- 1/4 cup unsweetened cocoa powder
- 1/4 cup coconut oil, melted
- 2 large eggs
- 1 teaspoon vanilla extract
- A pinch of salt

Instructions:

For the Crust:

1. Preheat your oven to 350°F (175°C). Line an 8x8-inch baking dish with parchment paper, leaving some overhang for easy removal.
2. In a mixing bowl, combine the almond flour, coconut flour, powdered erythritol, and salt.
3. Stir in the melted coconut oil and egg until a dough forms.
4. Press the dough evenly into the bottom of the prepared baking dish.
5. Bake the crust in the preheated oven for 10-12 minutes, or until lightly golden brown. Remove from the oven and let it cool slightly while you prepare the filling.

For the Filling:

1. In a separate mixing bowl, combine the chopped pecans, powdered erythritol, cocoa powder, melted coconut oil, eggs, vanilla extract, and a pinch of salt. Mix until well combined.

2. Pour the filling mixture over the partially baked crust, spreading it out evenly.
3. Return the dish to the oven and bake for an additional 20-25 minutes, or until the filling is set.
4. Once done, remove the baking dish from the oven and let the bars cool completely in the pan.
5. Once cooled, use the parchment paper overhang to lift the bars out of the pan. Place them on a cutting board and cut into squares or bars.
6. Store the sugar-free chocolate pecan pie bars in an airtight container at room temperature for up to 3 days, or in the refrigerator for longer shelf life. Enjoy these delicious bars as a guilt-free dessert!

These bars are perfect for satisfying your sweet cravings without the added sugar, making them a great option for those following a low-carb or sugar-free lifestyle.

Sugar-Free Chocolate Espresso Brownies

Ingredients:

- 1 cup almond flour
- 1/4 cup unsweetened cocoa powder
- 1/4 cup powdered erythritol or your preferred sugar-free sweetener
- 2 tablespoons finely ground espresso powder
- 1/2 teaspoon baking powder
- 1/4 teaspoon salt
- 1/2 cup unsweetened applesauce
- 1/4 cup coconut oil, melted
- 2 large eggs
- 1 teaspoon vanilla extract
- Optional: sugar-free chocolate chips for topping

Instructions:

1. Preheat your oven to 350°F (175°C). Grease or line an 8x8-inch baking pan with parchment paper, leaving some overhang for easy removal.
2. In a mixing bowl, whisk together the almond flour, cocoa powder, powdered erythritol, espresso powder, baking powder, and salt until well combined.
3. In another bowl, mix together the applesauce, melted coconut oil, eggs, and vanilla extract until smooth.
4. Gradually add the wet ingredients to the dry ingredients, stirring until a thick batter forms.
5. Pour the batter into the prepared baking pan, spreading it out evenly with a spatula.
6. If desired, sprinkle sugar-free chocolate chips over the top of the batter.
7. Bake in the preheated oven for 20-25 minutes, or until a toothpick inserted into the center comes out clean or with a few moist crumbs.
8. Once done, remove the brownies from the oven and let them cool in the pan for about 10 minutes.
9. Use the parchment paper overhang to lift the brownies out of the pan and transfer them to a wire rack to cool completely.
10. Once cooled, cut the brownies into squares or bars.
11. Store the sugar-free chocolate espresso brownies in an airtight container at room temperature for up to 3 days, or in the refrigerator for longer shelf life.

These brownies are rich, fudgy, and full of chocolate-espresso flavor, making them a perfect treat for any occasion. Enjoy them with a cup of coffee for an extra indulgent experience!

Sugar-Free Chocolate Coconut Bliss Balls

Ingredients:

- 1 cup unsweetened shredded coconut
- 1/4 cup unsweetened cocoa powder
- 1/4 cup almond flour
- 1/4 cup powdered erythritol or your preferred sugar-free sweetener
- 2 tablespoons coconut oil, melted
- 1 teaspoon vanilla extract
- A pinch of salt
- Unsweetened shredded coconut, cocoa powder, or chopped nuts for coating (optional)

Instructions:

1. In a food processor, combine the shredded coconut, cocoa powder, almond flour, powdered erythritol, melted coconut oil, vanilla extract, and a pinch of salt.
2. Pulse the mixture until it comes together into a sticky dough-like consistency.
3. If the mixture seems too dry, you can add a little more melted coconut oil or a splash of almond milk to help it stick together.
4. Once the mixture is well combined, use your hands to roll it into small balls, about 1 inch in diameter.
5. If desired, roll the balls in unsweetened shredded coconut, cocoa powder, or chopped nuts for an extra layer of flavor and texture.
6. Place the bliss balls on a baking sheet lined with parchment paper and refrigerate for at least 30 minutes to firm up.
7. Once firm, transfer the bliss balls to an airtight container and store them in the refrigerator for up to two weeks.

These sugar-free chocolate coconut bliss balls are perfect for satisfying your sweet cravings while still staying on track with your healthy eating goals. Enjoy them as a snack or dessert anytime you need a little pick-me-up!

Sugar-Free Chocolate Pumpkin Spice Cupcakes

Ingredients:

For the Cupcakes:

- 1 cup almond flour
- 1/4 cup unsweetened cocoa powder
- 1/4 cup powdered erythritol or your preferred sugar-free sweetener
- 1 teaspoon baking powder
- 1/2 teaspoon baking soda
- 1/4 teaspoon salt
- 1 teaspoon pumpkin spice blend
- 2 large eggs
- 1/2 cup pumpkin puree
- 1/4 cup coconut oil, melted
- 1 teaspoon vanilla extract

For the Frosting (optional):

- 1/2 cup unsalted butter, softened
- 1/4 cup powdered erythritol or your preferred sugar-free sweetener
- 1/4 cup cocoa powder
- 1/2 teaspoon vanilla extract
- 1/4 teaspoon pumpkin spice blend

Instructions:

For the Cupcakes:

1. Preheat your oven to 350°F (175°C). Line a muffin tin with cupcake liners or grease it well.
2. In a mixing bowl, whisk together the almond flour, cocoa powder, powdered erythritol, baking powder, baking soda, salt, and pumpkin spice blend until well combined.
3. In another bowl, beat the eggs, pumpkin puree, melted coconut oil, and vanilla extract until smooth.
4. Gradually add the wet ingredients to the dry ingredients, stirring until just combined. Be careful not to overmix.
5. Divide the batter evenly among the prepared muffin cups, filling each about 2/3 full.

6. Bake in the preheated oven for 18-22 minutes, or until a toothpick inserted into the center of a cupcake comes out clean.
7. Remove the cupcakes from the oven and let them cool in the pan for a few minutes before transferring them to a wire rack to cool completely.

For the Frosting (optional):

1. In a mixing bowl, beat the softened butter until creamy.
2. Gradually add the powdered erythritol, cocoa powder, vanilla extract, and pumpkin spice blend, beating until smooth and fluffy.
3. If the frosting is too thick, you can add a splash of milk or cream to reach your desired consistency.
4. Once the cupcakes are completely cooled, frost them with the chocolate pumpkin spice frosting using a piping bag or a knife.
5. Optionally, sprinkle additional pumpkin spice blend on top for garnish.
6. Store the frosted cupcakes in the refrigerator until ready to serve. Enjoy your sugar-free chocolate pumpkin spice cupcakes as a delightful autumn treat!

These cupcakes are perfect for Halloween parties, Thanksgiving gatherings, or any time you're craving a cozy fall dessert without the added sugar.

Sugar-Free Chocolate Avocado Brownies

Ingredients:

- 2 ripe avocados
- 1/2 cup unsweetened cocoa powder
- 1/2 cup almond flour
- 1/2 cup powdered erythritol or your preferred sugar-free sweetener
- 2 large eggs
- 1 teaspoon vanilla extract
- 1/2 teaspoon baking soda
- A pinch of salt
- Optional: sugar-free chocolate chips or chopped nuts for topping

Instructions:

1. Preheat your oven to 350°F (175°C). Grease or line an 8x8-inch baking pan with parchment paper.
2. In a food processor or blender, blend the avocados until smooth and creamy.
3. Add the cocoa powder, almond flour, powdered erythritol, eggs, vanilla extract, baking soda, and a pinch of salt to the blender with the avocado. Blend until everything is well combined and smooth.
4. Taste the batter and adjust sweetness if necessary by adding more sweetener.
5. Pour the batter into the prepared baking pan, spreading it out evenly with a spatula.
6. If desired, sprinkle sugar-free chocolate chips or chopped nuts on top of the batter.
7. Bake in the preheated oven for 25-30 minutes, or until the edges are set and a toothpick inserted into the center comes out with a few moist crumbs.
8. Remove the brownies from the oven and let them cool in the pan for at least 10 minutes before slicing.
9. Once cooled, cut the brownies into squares and serve. Enjoy your sugar-free chocolate avocado brownies as a guilt-free dessert or snack!

These brownies are perfect for those following a low-carb or ketogenic diet, and they're a great way to sneak in some extra nutrients from the avocado. Plus, the avocado adds a rich and creamy texture that pairs perfectly with the chocolate flavor.

Sugar-Free Chocolate Protein Smoothie Bowl

Ingredients:

For the Smoothie Bowl:

- 1 ripe banana, frozen
- 1/2 cup unsweetened almond milk or any milk of your choice
- 1 scoop chocolate protein powder (sugar-free)
- 1 tablespoon unsweetened cocoa powder
- 1 tablespoon almond butter or peanut butter (unsweetened)
- 1/2 teaspoon vanilla extract
- A handful of ice cubes

Toppings (optional):

- Sliced bananas
- Fresh berries (such as strawberries, raspberries)
- Unsweetened shredded coconut
- Chia seeds
- Chopped nuts (such as almonds, walnuts)
- Sugar-free granola or cereal

Instructions:

1. In a blender, combine the frozen banana, almond milk, chocolate protein powder, cocoa powder, almond butter, vanilla extract, and ice cubes.
2. Blend on high speed until smooth and creamy. If the mixture is too thick, you can add a little more almond milk to reach your desired consistency.
3. Once the smoothie mixture is smooth, pour it into a bowl.
4. Top the smoothie bowl with your favorite toppings. You can get creative here and add as many or as few toppings as you like.
5. Serve immediately and enjoy your sugar-free chocolate protein smoothie bowl with a spoon!

This smoothie bowl is not only delicious but also packed with protein, healthy fats, and fiber to keep you feeling full and satisfied. It's a great way to indulge your chocolate cravings without any added sugar. Plus, you can customize it with your favorite toppings for extra flavor and texture.

Sugar-Free Chocolate Almond Biscotti

Ingredients:

- 1 3/4 cups almond flour
- 1/4 cup unsweetened cocoa powder
- 1/4 cup powdered erythritol or your preferred sugar-free sweetener
- 1 teaspoon baking powder
- 1/4 teaspoon salt
- 1/2 cup unsalted almonds, chopped
- 2 large eggs
- 1 teaspoon vanilla extract
- 1/4 teaspoon almond extract (optional)

Instructions:

1. Preheat your oven to 325°F (160°C). Line a baking sheet with parchment paper.
2. In a large mixing bowl, combine the almond flour, cocoa powder, powdered erythritol, baking powder, and salt. Stir until well combined.
3. Add the chopped almonds to the dry ingredients and mix to distribute them evenly.
4. In a separate bowl, whisk together the eggs, vanilla extract, and almond extract (if using).
5. Pour the wet ingredients into the dry ingredients and mix until a dough forms. Use your hands to knead the dough a few times to ensure everything is well combined.
6. Transfer the dough onto the prepared baking sheet and shape it into a log, about 12 inches long and 3 inches wide. The dough will be sticky, so you can wet your hands slightly to help with shaping.
7. Bake the biscotti log in the preheated oven for 25-30 minutes, or until firm to the touch.
8. Remove the biscotti log from the oven and let it cool for about 10 minutes. Reduce the oven temperature to 300°F (150°C).
9. Using a sharp knife, carefully slice the biscotti log into 1/2-inch thick slices. Arrange the slices cut side down on the baking sheet.
10. Return the biscotti slices to the oven and bake for an additional 20-25 minutes, or until they are dry and crisp. You can flip them halfway through baking for even crisping.

11. Once done, remove the biscotti from the oven and let them cool completely on a wire rack.
12. Store the sugar-free chocolate almond biscotti in an airtight container at room temperature for up to two weeks. Enjoy them with a cup of coffee or tea for a delightful treat!

These biscotti are crunchy, chocolatey, and packed with almond flavor, making them a perfect snack or dessert option, especially for those looking to reduce their sugar intake.

Sugar-Free Chocolate Cherry Cheesecake Bites

Ingredients:

For the Crust:

- 1 cup almond flour
- 2 tablespoons unsweetened cocoa powder
- 2 tablespoons powdered erythritol or your preferred sugar-free sweetener
- 2 tablespoons coconut oil, melted

For the Cheesecake Filling:

- 8 oz (225g) cream cheese, softened
- 1/4 cup powdered erythritol or your preferred sugar-free sweetener
- 1/2 teaspoon vanilla extract
- 1 large egg

For the Chocolate Topping:

- 1/4 cup sugar-free chocolate chips
- 1/2 teaspoon coconut oil

For the Cherry Topping:

- 1/2 cup fresh cherries, pitted and halved

Instructions:

1. Preparing the Crust:

    1. Preheat your oven to 325°F (160°C). Line a mini muffin tin with paper liners or grease it lightly.
    2. In a mixing bowl, combine the almond flour, cocoa powder, powdered erythritol, and melted coconut oil. Stir until the mixture resembles coarse crumbs and holds together when pressed.
    3. Divide the mixture evenly among the mini muffin cups, pressing it down firmly to form the crust.
    4. Bake the crusts in the preheated oven for 10 minutes. Remove from the oven and let them cool slightly while you prepare the filling.

2. Making the Cheesecake Filling:

1. In a mixing bowl, beat the softened cream cheese, powdered erythritol, and vanilla extract until smooth and creamy.
2. Add the egg and beat until well combined and the mixture is smooth.

3. Assembling and Baking:

    1. Spoon the cheesecake filling over the cooled crusts, filling each cup almost to the top.
    2. Return the mini muffin tin to the oven and bake for 12-15 minutes, or until the cheesecake filling is set.
    3. Remove the cheesecake bites from the oven and let them cool completely in the muffin tin. Once cooled, transfer them to the refrigerator to chill for at least 1 hour.

4. Adding Toppings:

    1. In a small microwave-safe bowl, melt the sugar-free chocolate chips and coconut oil in the microwave in 30-second intervals, stirring in between until smooth.
    2. Drizzle the melted chocolate over the chilled cheesecake bites.
    3. Top each cheesecake bite with a halved cherry.

5. Serving:

    1. Serve the sugar-free chocolate cherry cheesecake bites chilled.
    2. Store any leftovers in an airtight container in the refrigerator for up to 3-4 days.

These sugar-free chocolate cherry cheesecake bites are perfect for satisfying your sweet cravings without the guilt. They're also great for serving at parties or as a special dessert for any occasion. Enjoy!

Sugar-Free Chocolate Peanut Butter Protein Bars

Ingredients:

For the Protein Bars:

- 1 cup almond flour
- 1/2 cup chocolate protein powder (sugar-free)
- 1/4 cup powdered erythritol or your preferred sugar-free sweetener
- 1/4 cup unsweetened cocoa powder
- 1/2 cup natural peanut butter (unsweetened)
- 1/4 cup coconut oil, melted
- 1 teaspoon vanilla extract
- A pinch of salt

For the Chocolate Coating:

- 1/4 cup sugar-free chocolate chips
- 1 tablespoon coconut oil

Instructions:

1. Making the Protein Bars:

    1. In a mixing bowl, combine the almond flour, chocolate protein powder, powdered erythritol, cocoa powder, peanut butter, melted coconut oil, vanilla extract, and a pinch of salt. Mix until well combined and a dough forms.
    2. Line an 8x8-inch baking dish with parchment paper, leaving some overhang for easy removal.
    3. Press the dough evenly into the bottom of the prepared baking dish.
    4. Place the baking dish in the refrigerator while you prepare the chocolate coating.

2. Adding the Chocolate Coating:

    1. In a small microwave-safe bowl, melt the sugar-free chocolate chips and coconut oil in the microwave in 30-second intervals, stirring in between until smooth.
    2. Remove the baking dish from the refrigerator and pour the melted chocolate mixture over the top of the dough, spreading it out evenly with a spatula.
    3. Return the baking dish to the refrigerator and chill for at least 1 hour, or until the chocolate coating is set.

3. Serving:

1. Once the chocolate coating is set, remove the protein bars from the refrigerator and lift them out of the baking dish using the parchment paper overhang.
2. Cut the bars into squares or rectangles using a sharp knife.
3. Store the sugar-free chocolate peanut butter protein bars in an airtight container in the refrigerator for up to one week.

These protein bars are perfect for a quick and satisfying snack on the go. They're packed with protein and healthy fats, making them a nutritious option for fueling your day. Enjoy!

Sugar-Free Chocolate Oatmeal Cookies

Ingredients:

- 1 cup rolled oats
- 1/2 cup almond flour
- 1/4 cup unsweetened cocoa powder
- 1/4 cup powdered erythritol or your preferred sugar-free sweetener
- 1/2 teaspoon baking powder
- 1/4 teaspoon salt
- 1/4 cup coconut oil, melted
- 1 large egg
- 1 teaspoon vanilla extract
- 1/4 cup sugar-free chocolate chips (optional)

Instructions:

1. Preheat your oven to 350°F (175°C). Line a baking sheet with parchment paper or lightly grease it.
2. In a large mixing bowl, combine the rolled oats, almond flour, cocoa powder, powdered erythritol, baking powder, and salt. Stir until well combined.
3. In a separate bowl, whisk together the melted coconut oil, egg, and vanilla extract until smooth.
4. Pour the wet ingredients into the dry ingredients and mix until a dough forms. If using, fold in the sugar-free chocolate chips.
5. Scoop tablespoon-sized portions of dough onto the prepared baking sheet, spacing them about 2 inches apart. Use your hands to flatten each cookie slightly.
6. Bake in the preheated oven for 10-12 minutes, or until the edges are set. The cookies will still be soft in the middle.
7. Remove the cookies from the oven and let them cool on the baking sheet for a few minutes before transferring them to a wire rack to cool completely.
8. Once cooled, store the sugar-free chocolate oatmeal cookies in an airtight container at room temperature for up to one week.

These cookies are perfect for satisfying your sweet cravings without the added sugar. Enjoy them as a guilt-free snack or dessert!

Sugar-Free Chocolate Chia Seed Pudding Parfait

Ingredients:

For the Chocolate Chia Seed Pudding:

- 1/4 cup chia seeds
- 1 cup unsweetened almond milk or any milk of your choice
- 2 tablespoons unsweetened cocoa powder
- 1-2 tablespoons powdered erythritol or your preferred sugar-free sweetener
- 1/2 teaspoon vanilla extract
- A pinch of salt

For the Parfait Layers:

- Sugar-free Greek yogurt or coconut yogurt
- Sugar-free whipped cream or coconut whipped cream
- Fresh berries (such as strawberries, raspberries)
- Unsweetened shredded coconut or chopped nuts for garnish (optional)

Instructions:

1. Making the Chocolate Chia Seed Pudding:

    1. In a mixing bowl, whisk together the chia seeds, almond milk, unsweetened cocoa powder, powdered erythritol, vanilla extract, and a pinch of salt until well combined.
    2. Let the mixture sit for about 5 minutes, then whisk again to prevent clumps from forming.
    3. Cover the bowl and refrigerate the chocolate chia seed pudding mixture for at least 2 hours, or preferably overnight, to thicken.

2. Assembling the Parfait:

    1. Once the chocolate chia seed pudding has thickened, it's time to assemble the parfait.
    2. In serving glasses or jars, alternate layers of the chocolate chia seed pudding with layers of sugar-free Greek yogurt or coconut yogurt.
    3. Continue layering until the glasses are filled to your liking, ending with a layer of pudding on top.

4. Top each parfait with a dollop of sugar-free whipped cream or coconut whipped cream.
5. Garnish the parfaits with fresh berries and a sprinkle of unsweetened shredded coconut or chopped nuts, if desired.
6. Serve immediately, or cover and refrigerate until ready to serve.

3. Serving:

1. Enjoy your sugar-free chocolate chia seed pudding parfait as a nutritious breakfast, snack, or dessert.
2. Feel free to customize your parfait with additional toppings such as sugar-free chocolate chips, sliced almonds, or a drizzle of sugar-free chocolate sauce.

This chocolate chia seed pudding parfait is not only delicious but also packed with protein, fiber, and healthy fats, making it a perfect guilt-free treat for any time of day!

Sugar-Free Chocolate Hazelnut Torte

Ingredients:

For the Torte:

- 1 cup hazelnut meal or ground hazelnuts
- 1/2 cup almond flour
- 1/4 cup unsweetened cocoa powder
- 1/4 cup powdered erythritol or your preferred sugar-free sweetener
- 1/2 teaspoon baking powder
- 1/4 teaspoon salt
- 1/2 cup unsweetened applesauce
- 1/4 cup coconut oil, melted
- 3 large eggs
- 1 teaspoon vanilla extract

For the Chocolate Ganache:

- 1/2 cup sugar-free chocolate chips
- 1/4 cup heavy cream or coconut cream

For Garnish (optional):

- Chopped hazelnuts
- Sugar-free whipped cream

Instructions:

1. Preparing the Torte:

   1. Preheat your oven to 350°F (175°C). Grease an 8-inch round cake pan and line the bottom with parchment paper.
   2. In a mixing bowl, combine the hazelnut meal, almond flour, cocoa powder, powdered erythritol, baking powder, and salt. Stir until well combined.
   3. In another bowl, whisk together the unsweetened applesauce, melted coconut oil, eggs, and vanilla extract until smooth.
   4. Gradually add the wet ingredients to the dry ingredients, stirring until a smooth batter forms.
   5. Pour the batter into the prepared cake pan and spread it out evenly with a spatula.

6. Bake in the preheated oven for 25-30 minutes, or until a toothpick inserted into the center comes out clean.
7. Remove the torte from the oven and let it cool in the pan for about 10 minutes before transferring it to a wire rack to cool completely.

2. Making the Chocolate Ganache:

1. In a small saucepan, heat the heavy cream over medium heat until it just begins to simmer. Remove from heat.
2. Place the sugar-free chocolate chips in a heatproof bowl. Pour the hot cream over the chocolate chips and let it sit for 1-2 minutes.
3. Stir the chocolate and cream together until smooth and glossy, forming a ganache.

3. Assembling the Torte:

1. Once the torte has cooled completely, transfer it to a serving platter.
2. Pour the chocolate ganache over the top of the torte, allowing it to drip down the sides.
3. Garnish the torte with chopped hazelnuts and/or sugar-free whipped cream, if desired.
4. Slice and serve the sugar-free chocolate hazelnut torte. Enjoy!

This indulgent dessert is rich in flavor and perfect for special occasions or whenever you're craving something sweet without the added sugar.

Sugar-Free Chocolate Coconut Flour Pancakes

Ingredients:

- 1/4 cup coconut flour
- 2 tablespoons unsweetened cocoa powder
- 1/4 teaspoon baking powder
- 1/4 teaspoon salt
- 4 large eggs
- 1/4 cup unsweetened almond milk or any milk of your choice
- 2 tablespoons powdered erythritol or your preferred sugar-free sweetener
- 1 teaspoon vanilla extract
- Coconut oil or butter for cooking

Instructions:

1. In a mixing bowl, whisk together the coconut flour, cocoa powder, baking powder, and salt until well combined.
2. In another bowl, whisk together the eggs, almond milk, powdered erythritol, and vanilla extract until smooth.
3. Gradually add the wet ingredients to the dry ingredients, stirring until a smooth batter forms. Let the batter sit for a few minutes to allow the coconut flour to absorb the liquids.
4. Heat a non-stick skillet or griddle over medium heat and lightly grease it with coconut oil or butter.
5. Pour about 1/4 cup of batter onto the skillet for each pancake, spreading it out slightly with the back of a spoon to form a round shape.
6. Cook the pancakes for 2-3 minutes, or until bubbles form on the surface and the edges start to look set.
7. Carefully flip the pancakes and cook for an additional 1-2 minutes on the other side, or until cooked through.
8. Repeat with the remaining batter, greasing the skillet as needed between batches.
9. Serve the sugar-free chocolate coconut flour pancakes warm with your favorite toppings, such as sugar-free maple syrup, fresh berries, sliced bananas, or sugar-free whipped cream.

These pancakes are fluffy, chocolatey, and perfect for a delicious and guilt-free breakfast or brunch!

Sugar-Free Chocolate Cashew Cheesecake

Ingredients:

For the Crust:

- 1 cup almond flour
- 1/4 cup unsweetened cocoa powder
- 2 tablespoons powdered erythritol or your preferred sugar-free sweetener
- 1/4 cup coconut oil, melted

For the Filling:

- 2 cups raw cashews, soaked in water for at least 4 hours or overnight, then drained
- 1/2 cup unsweetened coconut cream
- 1/4 cup powdered erythritol or your preferred sugar-free sweetener
- 1/4 cup unsweetened cocoa powder
- 1/4 cup coconut oil, melted
- 2 tablespoons lemon juice
- 1 teaspoon vanilla extract
- A pinch of salt

For the Chocolate Ganache:

- 1/2 cup sugar-free chocolate chips
- 1/4 cup unsweetened coconut cream
- 1 tablespoon powdered erythritol or your preferred sugar-free sweetener

Instructions:

1. Making the Crust:

    1. Preheat your oven to 350°F (175°C). Grease a 9-inch springform pan and line the bottom with parchment paper.
    2. In a mixing bowl, combine the almond flour, cocoa powder, powdered erythritol, and melted coconut oil. Stir until well combined and the mixture resembles coarse crumbs.
    3. Press the mixture firmly into the bottom of the prepared springform pan, forming an even layer.

4. Bake the crust in the preheated oven for 10-12 minutes, or until set. Remove from the oven and let it cool while you prepare the filling.

2. Making the Filling:

1. In a food processor or high-powered blender, combine the soaked and drained cashews, coconut cream, powdered erythritol, cocoa powder, melted coconut oil, lemon juice, vanilla extract, and a pinch of salt.
2. Blend the mixture until smooth and creamy, scraping down the sides of the bowl as needed to ensure everything is well combined.
3. Taste the filling and adjust sweetness or flavorings as desired.
4. Pour the filling over the cooled crust in the springform pan, smoothing it out into an even layer with a spatula.
5. Place the cheesecake in the freezer to set while you prepare the chocolate ganache.

3. Making the Chocolate Ganache:

1. In a small saucepan, heat the coconut cream over medium heat until it just begins to simmer.
2. Place the sugar-free chocolate chips and powdered erythritol in a heatproof bowl. Pour the hot coconut cream over the chocolate chips and let it sit for 1-2 minutes.
3. Stir the chocolate and coconut cream together until smooth and glossy, forming a ganache.

4. Assembling the Cheesecake:

1. Remove the cheesecake from the freezer and pour the chocolate ganache over the top, spreading it out into an even layer with a spatula.
2. Return the cheesecake to the freezer to set for at least 4 hours, or preferably overnight.
3. Before serving, let the cheesecake sit at room temperature for about 10-15 minutes to soften slightly.
4. Garnish the cheesecake with additional chopped nuts or shaved chocolate, if desired.
5. Slice and serve your sugar-free chocolate cashew cheesecake chilled. Enjoy!

This cheesecake is rich, creamy, and decadently chocolatey, making it a perfect treat for special occasions or any time you're craving a delicious dessert without the added sugar.

Sugar-Free Chocolate Banana Ice Cream

Ingredients:

- 3 ripe bananas, peeled, sliced, and frozen
- 2 tablespoons unsweetened cocoa powder
- 1 teaspoon vanilla extract
- 1/4 cup unsweetened almond milk or any milk of your choice (optional, for easier blending)
- Sugar-free sweetener to taste (optional)

Instructions:

1. Place the frozen banana slices in a food processor or high-powered blender.
2. Add the unsweetened cocoa powder and vanilla extract to the blender.
3. If using, pour in the unsweetened almond milk to help with blending.
4. Blend the mixture until smooth and creamy, scraping down the sides of the blender as needed. If the mixture is too thick, you can add more almond milk, a tablespoon at a time, until you reach your desired consistency.
5. Taste the ice cream and add sugar-free sweetener, such as powdered erythritol or stevia, if desired. Blend again until well combined.
6. Once the ice cream is smooth and sweetened to your liking, transfer it to a freezer-safe container and freeze for at least 1-2 hours to firm up before serving.
7. Before serving, let the ice cream sit at room temperature for a few minutes to soften slightly, making it easier to scoop.
8. Scoop the sugar-free chocolate banana ice cream into bowls or cones and enjoy it as a delicious and guilt-free dessert!

This ice cream is naturally sweet from the bananas and has a rich chocolate flavor, making it a healthier alternative to traditional ice cream. Feel free to customize it by adding in extras like sugar-free chocolate chips, chopped nuts, or a drizzle of sugar-free chocolate sauce.

Sugar-Free Chocolate Almond Joy Bites

Ingredients:

For the Coconut Filling:

- 1 cup unsweetened shredded coconut
- 2 tablespoons coconut oil, melted
- 2 tablespoons powdered erythritol or your preferred sugar-free sweetener
- 1/2 teaspoon vanilla extract
- 1/4 teaspoon almond extract (optional)
- Pinch of salt

For the Chocolate Coating:

- 1/2 cup sugar-free chocolate chips
- 1 tablespoon coconut oil

For Garnish (optional):

- Whole almonds

Instructions:

1. Making the Coconut Filling:

    1. In a mixing bowl, combine the unsweetened shredded coconut, melted coconut oil, powdered erythritol, vanilla extract, almond extract (if using), and a pinch of salt. Stir until well combined.
    2. Using your hands, shape the coconut mixture into small bite-sized balls or oblong shapes, similar to the size and shape of almond joy candies. Place them on a baking sheet lined with parchment paper.
    3. If desired, press a whole almond into the top of each coconut bite, resembling the almond found in almond joy candies.
    4. Place the baking sheet in the refrigerator to chill the coconut filling while you prepare the chocolate coating.

2. Making the Chocolate Coating:

    1. In a small saucepan or microwave-safe bowl, melt the sugar-free chocolate chips and coconut oil together until smooth and glossy, stirring frequently to prevent burning.

2. Once melted, remove the saucepan from the heat or bowl from the microwave.

3. Assembling the Almond Joy Bites:

1. Remove the chilled coconut filling from the refrigerator.
2. Using a fork or toothpick, dip each coconut bite into the melted chocolate coating, ensuring it is evenly coated.
3. Tap off any excess chocolate and place the coated coconut bite back onto the parchment-lined baking sheet.
4. Once all the coconut bites are coated in chocolate, return the baking sheet to the refrigerator to allow the chocolate coating to set, about 15-20 minutes.
5. Once the chocolate coating is firm, transfer the sugar-free chocolate almond joy bites to an airtight container and store them in the refrigerator until ready to serve.

These sugar-free chocolate almond joy bites are a delightful treat that captures the flavors of the classic candy bar without the added sugar. Enjoy them as a guilt-free indulgence whenever you're craving something sweet!

Sugar-Free Chocolate Raspberry Coconut Bars

Ingredients:

For the Coconut Layer:

- 2 cups unsweetened shredded coconut
- 1/4 cup coconut oil, melted
- 1/4 cup powdered erythritol or your preferred sugar-free sweetener
- 1 teaspoon vanilla extract
- Pinch of salt

For the Raspberry Filling:

- 1 cup fresh raspberries
- 1 tablespoon water
- 1 tablespoon powdered erythritol or your preferred sugar-free sweetener

For the Chocolate Coating:

- 1/2 cup sugar-free chocolate chips
- 1 tablespoon coconut oil

Instructions:

1. Making the Coconut Layer:

   1. In a mixing bowl, combine the unsweetened shredded coconut, melted coconut oil, powdered erythritol, vanilla extract, and a pinch of salt. Stir until well combined.
   2. Line a square baking dish with parchment paper, leaving some overhang for easy removal.
   3. Press the coconut mixture firmly into the bottom of the prepared baking dish, forming an even layer.
   4. Place the baking dish in the refrigerator to chill while you prepare the raspberry filling.

2. Making the Raspberry Filling:

   1. In a small saucepan, combine the fresh raspberries, water, and powdered erythritol over medium heat.

2. Cook the mixture, stirring occasionally, until the raspberries break down and the mixture thickens, about 5-7 minutes.
3. Once thickened, remove the raspberry filling from the heat and let it cool slightly.
4. Once cooled, pour the raspberry filling over the chilled coconut layer in the baking dish, spreading it out into an even layer.
5. Return the baking dish to the refrigerator to chill while you prepare the chocolate coating.

3. Making the Chocolate Coating:

1. In a small saucepan or microwave-safe bowl, melt the sugar-free chocolate chips and coconut oil together until smooth and glossy, stirring frequently to prevent burning.
2. Once melted, remove the saucepan from the heat or bowl from the microwave.

4. Assembling the Bars:

1. Remove the chilled baking dish from the refrigerator.
2. Pour the melted chocolate coating over the raspberry layer, spreading it out evenly with a spatula.
3. Return the baking dish to the refrigerator and chill until the chocolate coating is set, about 1-2 hours.
4. Once set, lift the parchment paper to remove the bars from the baking dish. Place them on a cutting board and slice into squares or bars.
5. Serve your sugar-free chocolate raspberry coconut bars chilled and enjoy!

These bars are a delightful combination of flavors and textures, making them a perfect treat for any occasion. Plus, they're sugar-free, so you can indulge without the guilt!

Sugar-Free Chocolate Pecan Pralines

Ingredients:

- 1 cup chopped pecans
- 1/2 cup powdered erythritol or your preferred sugar-free sweetener
- 1/4 cup unsweetened cocoa powder
- 1/4 cup heavy cream
- 2 tablespoons unsalted butter
- 1 teaspoon vanilla extract
- Pinch of salt

Instructions:

1. Preparing the Pecans:

    1. Preheat your oven to 350°F (175°C). Spread the chopped pecans evenly on a baking sheet lined with parchment paper.
    2. Toast the pecans in the preheated oven for 5-7 minutes, or until they are fragrant and lightly browned. Keep an eye on them to prevent burning. Remove from the oven and let them cool while you prepare the praline mixture.

2. Making the Praline Mixture:

    1. In a saucepan over medium heat, combine the powdered erythritol, unsweetened cocoa powder, heavy cream, and unsalted butter.
    2. Cook the mixture, stirring constantly, until the butter is melted and the ingredients are well combined.
    3. Continue to cook the mixture, stirring frequently, until it thickens slightly and reaches a soft ball stage, about 5-7 minutes. You can test the consistency by dropping a small amount of the mixture into a bowl of cold water. It should form a soft ball that holds its shape but is still pliable.
    4. Once the mixture reaches the soft ball stage, remove the saucepan from the heat.
    5. Stir in the vanilla extract and a pinch of salt until well combined.

3. Adding the Pecans:

    1. Quickly stir in the toasted chopped pecans until they are evenly coated with the praline mixture.

4. Shaping the Pralines:

   1. Drop spoonfuls of the praline mixture onto a baking sheet lined with parchment paper, spacing them apart to allow room for spreading.
   2. Let the pralines cool and set at room temperature for about 30 minutes, or until firm.
   3. Once set, transfer the sugar-free chocolate pecan pralines to an airtight container and store them in the refrigerator until ready to serve.

These sugar-free chocolate pecan pralines are a decadent treat that's perfect for satisfying your sweet cravings without the added sugar. Enjoy them as a delicious snack or dessert!

Sugar-Free Chocolate Chia Seed Energy Balls

Ingredients:

- 1 cup pitted dates, soaked in warm water for 10 minutes and drained
- 1/4 cup unsweetened cocoa powder
- 1/4 cup almond butter or peanut butter (unsweetened)
- 1/4 cup chia seeds
- 1 teaspoon vanilla extract
- Pinch of salt
- Optional add-ins: chopped nuts, unsweetened shredded coconut, sugar-free chocolate chips

Instructions:

1. In a food processor, combine the soaked dates, unsweetened cocoa powder, almond butter or peanut butter, chia seeds, vanilla extract, and a pinch of salt.
2. Pulse the mixture until it forms a thick and sticky dough. If the mixture is too dry, you can add a teaspoon of water at a time until it reaches the desired consistency.
3. If using optional add-ins like chopped nuts or unsweetened shredded coconut, fold them into the dough until evenly distributed.
4. Once the dough is ready, scoop out tablespoon-sized portions and roll them into balls using your hands.
5. Place the chocolate chia seed energy balls on a baking sheet lined with parchment paper.
6. Refrigerate the energy balls for at least 30 minutes to allow them to firm up.
7. Once firm, transfer the energy balls to an airtight container and store them in the refrigerator for up to one week.

These sugar-free chocolate chia seed energy balls are packed with nutrients and make a delicious and convenient snack to have on hand for a quick energy boost throughout the day!

Sugar-Free Chocolate Coconut Flour Brownies

Ingredients:

- 1/2 cup coconut flour
- 1/2 cup unsweetened cocoa powder
- 1/2 cup powdered erythritol or your preferred sugar-free sweetener
- 1/2 teaspoon baking powder
- 1/4 teaspoon salt
- 1/2 cup unsalted butter, melted
- 4 large eggs
- 1 teaspoon vanilla extract
- 1/4 cup unsweetened almond milk or any milk of your choice

Instructions:

1. Preheat your oven to 350°F (175°C). Grease an 8x8 inch baking pan or line it with parchment paper for easy removal.
2. In a mixing bowl, sift together the coconut flour, cocoa powder, powdered erythritol, baking powder, and salt. Ensure there are no lumps and the dry ingredients are well combined.
3. In another mixing bowl, whisk together the melted butter, eggs, vanilla extract, and unsweetened almond milk until smooth and well combined.
4. Gradually add the dry ingredients to the wet ingredients, stirring until a thick batter forms and there are no dry spots.
5. Pour the batter into the prepared baking pan and spread it out evenly with a spatula.
6. Bake in the preheated oven for 20-25 minutes, or until the brownies are set and a toothpick inserted into the center comes out with a few moist crumbs.
7. Remove the brownies from the oven and let them cool in the pan for about 10 minutes before slicing and serving.
8. Once cooled, slice the brownies into squares and serve. Enjoy your sugar-free chocolate coconut flour brownies!

These brownies are perfect for anyone looking for a low-carb or sugar-free treat without sacrificing on flavor or texture. They're great for satisfying chocolate cravings while still sticking to a healthy eating plan.

Sugar-Free Chocolate Peanut Butter Energy Bites

Ingredients:

- 1 cup old-fashioned oats
- 1/2 cup unsweetened cocoa powder
- 1/2 cup natural peanut butter (unsweetened)
- 1/4 cup powdered erythritol or your preferred sugar-free sweetener
- 1/4 cup unsweetened almond milk or any milk of your choice
- 1 teaspoon vanilla extract
- Pinch of salt
- Optional add-ins: chopped nuts, sugar-free chocolate chips, chia seeds, flaxseeds, shredded coconut

Instructions:

1. In a large mixing bowl, combine the old-fashioned oats, unsweetened cocoa powder, powdered erythritol, and a pinch of salt. Stir until well combined.
2. Add the natural peanut butter, unsweetened almond milk, and vanilla extract to the dry ingredients. Stir until a thick dough forms.
3. If using optional add-ins like chopped nuts or sugar-free chocolate chips, fold them into the dough until evenly distributed.
4. Once the dough is ready, scoop out tablespoon-sized portions and roll them into balls using your hands.
5. Place the chocolate peanut butter energy bites on a baking sheet lined with parchment paper.
6. Refrigerate the energy bites for at least 30 minutes to allow them to firm up.
7. Once firm, transfer the energy bites to an airtight container and store them in the refrigerator for up to one week.

These sugar-free chocolate peanut butter energy bites are packed with protein and fiber, making them a perfect snack for a quick energy boost throughout the day!

Sugar-Free Chocolate Cherry Smoothie

Ingredients:

- 1 cup unsweetened almond milk or any milk of your choice
- 1 cup frozen cherries, pitted
- 1 tablespoon unsweetened cocoa powder
- 1 tablespoon almond butter or peanut butter (unsweetened)
- 1/2 teaspoon vanilla extract
- 1/2 cup plain Greek yogurt or coconut yogurt
- Optional: 1-2 tablespoons powdered erythritol or your preferred sugar-free sweetener, to taste
- Ice cubes (optional, for a thicker smoothie)

Instructions:

1. Place all the ingredients in a blender.
2. Blend until smooth and creamy, scraping down the sides of the blender as needed.
3. Taste the smoothie and adjust sweetness by adding powdered erythritol or your preferred sugar-free sweetener, if desired.
4. If you prefer a thicker smoothie, you can add a handful of ice cubes and blend again until smooth.
5. Once blended to your desired consistency, pour the sugar-free chocolate cherry smoothie into glasses and serve immediately.

This smoothie is not only delicious but also packed with antioxidants from the cherries and protein from the Greek yogurt, making it a nutritious and refreshing treat any time of day!

Sugar-Free Chocolate Coconut Cream Pie

Ingredients:

For the Crust:

- 1 1/2 cups almond flour
- 1/4 cup unsweetened cocoa powder
- 2 tablespoons powdered erythritol or your preferred sugar-free sweetener
- 1/4 cup coconut oil, melted
- Pinch of salt

For the Coconut Cream Filling:

- 1 can (13.5 oz) full-fat coconut milk
- 1/4 cup powdered erythritol or your preferred sugar-free sweetener
- 2 tablespoons coconut flour
- 1 teaspoon vanilla extract
- 1/2 cup unsweetened shredded coconut

For the Chocolate Ganache Topping:

- 1/2 cup sugar-free chocolate chips
- 1/4 cup heavy cream or coconut cream
- Unsweetened shredded coconut, for garnish (optional)

Instructions:

1. Making the Crust:

   1. Preheat your oven to 350°F (175°C).
   2. In a mixing bowl, combine the almond flour, cocoa powder, powdered erythritol, melted coconut oil, and a pinch of salt. Mix until well combined and the mixture resembles coarse crumbs.
   3. Press the mixture firmly into the bottom and up the sides of a 9-inch pie dish.
   4. Bake the crust in the preheated oven for 10-12 minutes, or until set. Remove from the oven and let it cool completely.

2. Making the Coconut Cream Filling:

   1. In a saucepan, combine the full-fat coconut milk and powdered erythritol over medium heat. Whisk until the erythritol is dissolved.

2. Add the coconut flour and vanilla extract to the saucepan, whisking constantly to prevent lumps.
3. Cook the mixture, stirring frequently, until it thickens, about 5-7 minutes.
4. Once thickened, remove the saucepan from the heat and stir in the unsweetened shredded coconut.
5. Pour the coconut cream filling into the cooled crust, spreading it out into an even layer. Refrigerate while you prepare the chocolate ganache topping.

3. Making the Chocolate Ganache Topping:

1. In a small saucepan, heat the heavy cream over medium heat until it just begins to simmer.
2. Place the sugar-free chocolate chips in a heatproof bowl. Pour the hot cream over the chocolate chips and let it sit for 1-2 minutes.
3. Stir the chocolate and cream together until smooth and glossy, forming a ganache.

4. Assembling the Pie:

1. Pour the chocolate ganache over the coconut cream filling, spreading it out into an even layer with a spatula.
2. If desired, sprinkle unsweetened shredded coconut over the top of the ganache for garnish.
3. Refrigerate the chocolate coconut cream pie for at least 2 hours, or until set.
4. Once set, slice and serve your sugar-free chocolate coconut cream pie chilled. Enjoy!

This pie is rich, creamy, and full of chocolate and coconut flavor, making it a perfect dessert for any occasion, without the added sugar.

Sugar-Free Chocolate Macadamia Nut Cookies

Ingredients:

- 1 cup almond flour
- 1/4 cup unsweetened cocoa powder
- 1/4 cup powdered erythritol or your preferred sugar-free sweetener
- 1/2 teaspoon baking powder
- Pinch of salt
- 1/4 cup coconut oil, melted
- 1 large egg
- 1 teaspoon vanilla extract
- 1/2 cup chopped macadamia nuts
- 1/4 cup sugar-free chocolate chips

Instructions:

1. Preheat your oven to 350°F (175°C). Line a baking sheet with parchment paper or silicone baking mat.
2. In a mixing bowl, combine the almond flour, unsweetened cocoa powder, powdered erythritol, baking powder, and a pinch of salt. Mix until well combined.
3. In a separate bowl, whisk together the melted coconut oil, egg, and vanilla extract until smooth.
4. Pour the wet ingredients into the dry ingredients and mix until a thick cookie dough forms.
5. Fold in the chopped macadamia nuts and sugar-free chocolate chips until evenly distributed throughout the dough.
6. Using a cookie scoop or spoon, drop tablespoon-sized portions of dough onto the prepared baking sheet, spacing them about 2 inches apart.
7. Flatten each cookie slightly with the back of a spoon or your fingers.
8. Bake in the preheated oven for 10-12 minutes, or until the edges are set and the tops are slightly firm to the touch.
9. Remove the cookies from the oven and let them cool on the baking sheet for a few minutes before transferring them to a wire rack to cool completely.
10. Once cooled, store the sugar-free chocolate macadamia nut cookies in an airtight container at room temperature for up to one week.

These cookies are perfect for anyone looking for a delicious treat without the added sugar. Enjoy them with a glass of milk or your favorite hot beverage for a delightful snack or dessert!

Sugar-Free Chocolate Pistachio Truffles

Ingredients:

For the Truffles:

- 1 cup shelled pistachios
- 1 cup sugar-free chocolate chips
- 1/2 cup coconut cream (the thick, creamy part from a can of full-fat coconut milk)
- 1 teaspoon vanilla extract
- Pinch of salt

For Coating (Optional):

- Crushed pistachios
- Unsweetened cocoa powder
- Unsweetened shredded coconut

Instructions:

1. Toasting the Pistachios:

   1. Preheat your oven to 350°F (175°C).
   2. Spread the shelled pistachios on a baking sheet lined with parchment paper.
   3. Toast the pistachios in the preheated oven for 8-10 minutes, or until lightly golden and fragrant. Keep an eye on them to prevent burning. Remove from the oven and let them cool.

2. Making the Truffle Mixture:

   1. In a food processor, pulse the toasted pistachios until finely ground. Set aside.
   2. In a microwave-safe bowl or a small saucepan, melt the sugar-free chocolate chips and coconut cream together until smooth and creamy. Stir in the vanilla extract and a pinch of salt.
   3. Add the ground pistachios to the melted chocolate mixture and stir until well combined.
   4. Place the mixture in the refrigerator to firm up for about 1-2 hours, or until it's easy to handle and shape into balls.

3. Shaping the Truffles:

1. Once the mixture is firm, use a spoon or a small cookie scoop to portion out small amounts of the mixture.
2. Roll each portion into a ball between your palms to form the truffles.

4. Coating the Truffles (Optional):

1. Roll each truffle in your choice of coating, such as crushed pistachios, unsweetened cocoa powder, or unsweetened shredded coconut, until evenly coated.
2. Place the coated truffles on a baking sheet lined with parchment paper.
3. Once all the truffles are coated, refrigerate them for another 30 minutes to firm up.

5. Serving and Storage:

1. Serve the sugar-free chocolate pistachio truffles chilled. Enjoy!
2. Store any leftover truffles in an airtight container in the refrigerator for up to one week.

These sugar-free chocolate pistachio truffles make for an elegant and indulgent treat, perfect for special occasions or as a homemade gift for friends and family!

Sugar-Free Chocolate Raspberry Cake Roll

Ingredients:

For the Cake:

- 4 large eggs, separated
- 1/2 cup powdered erythritol or your preferred sugar-free sweetener, divided
- 1 teaspoon vanilla extract
- 1/4 cup unsweetened cocoa powder
- 1/4 cup almond flour
- 1 teaspoon baking powder
- Pinch of salt

For the Filling:

- 1 cup fresh raspberries
- 1 cup heavy cream, chilled
- 2 tablespoons powdered erythritol or your preferred sugar-free sweetener
- 1 teaspoon vanilla extract

For the Ganache:

- 1/2 cup sugar-free chocolate chips
- 1/4 cup heavy cream

Instructions:

1. Making the Cake:

   1. Preheat your oven to 350°F (175°C). Grease a 10x15-inch jelly roll pan and line it with parchment paper.
   2. In a large mixing bowl, beat the egg whites with an electric mixer until soft peaks form. Gradually add half of the powdered erythritol and continue to beat until stiff peaks form.
   3. In another mixing bowl, beat the egg yolks with the remaining powdered erythritol and vanilla extract until pale and fluffy.
   4. Sift in the cocoa powder, almond flour, baking powder, and a pinch of salt into the egg yolk mixture. Gently fold until just combined.
   5. Carefully fold the beaten egg whites into the cocoa mixture until no streaks remain.

6. Spread the batter evenly into the prepared jelly roll pan.
7. Bake in the preheated oven for 10-12 minutes, or until the cake is set and springs back when lightly touched.
8. Remove the cake from the oven and let it cool in the pan for a few minutes.
9. While the cake is still warm, gently roll it up with the parchment paper from the short end. Transfer the rolled cake to a wire rack to cool completely.

2. Making the Filling:

   1. In a mixing bowl, whip the chilled heavy cream with powdered erythritol and vanilla extract until stiff peaks form.
   2. Gently fold in the fresh raspberries until evenly distributed.

3. Assembling the Cake Roll:

   1. Carefully unroll the cooled cake and remove the parchment paper.
   2. Spread the whipped cream and raspberry filling evenly over the cake, leaving a small border around the edges.
   3. Gently roll the cake back up, without the parchment paper this time. Place seam side down on a serving platter.

4. Making the Ganache:

   1. In a small saucepan, heat the heavy cream over medium heat until it just begins to simmer.
   2. Place the sugar-free chocolate chips in a heatproof bowl. Pour the hot cream over the chocolate chips and let it sit for 1-2 minutes.
   3. Stir the chocolate and cream together until smooth and glossy, forming a ganache.

5. Decorating the Cake Roll:

   1. Pour the ganache over the top of the cake roll, allowing it to drip down the sides.
   2. Refrigerate the cake roll for at least 30 minutes to allow the ganache to set.
   3. Before serving, garnish the cake roll with fresh raspberries and a dusting of powdered erythritol, if desired.
   4. Slice and serve your sugar-free chocolate raspberry cake roll chilled. Enjoy!

This cake roll is a delightful combination of rich chocolate cake, creamy raspberry filling, and decadent chocolate ganache, making it a perfect dessert for any occasion!

Sugar-Free Chocolate Orange Cheesecake

Ingredients:

For the Crust:

- 1 1/2 cups almond flour
- 1/4 cup unsweetened cocoa powder
- 1/4 cup powdered erythritol or your preferred sugar-free sweetener
- 1/4 cup unsalted butter, melted
- Pinch of salt

For the Cheesecake Filling:

- 24 oz (3 packages) cream cheese, softened
- 1 cup powdered erythritol or your preferred sugar-free sweetener
- 3 large eggs
- 1/2 cup sour cream
- 1/4 cup heavy cream
- Zest of 1 orange
- 2 tablespoons freshly squeezed orange juice
- 1 teaspoon vanilla extract
- Pinch of salt

For the Chocolate Ganache Topping:

- 1/2 cup sugar-free chocolate chips
- 1/4 cup heavy cream
- Zest of 1 orange, for garnish (optional)

Instructions:

1. Making the Crust:

    1. Preheat your oven to 325°F (160°C). Grease a 9-inch springform pan and line the bottom with parchment paper.
    2. In a mixing bowl, combine the almond flour, cocoa powder, powdered erythritol, melted butter, and a pinch of salt. Stir until well combined and the mixture resembles coarse crumbs.
    3. Press the mixture firmly into the bottom of the prepared springform pan, forming an even layer.

4. Bake the crust in the preheated oven for 10-12 minutes, or until set. Remove from the oven and let it cool while you prepare the cheesecake filling.

2. Making the Cheesecake Filling:

   1. In a large mixing bowl, beat the softened cream cheese and powdered erythritol together until smooth and creamy.
   2. Add the eggs, one at a time, beating well after each addition.
   3. Add the sour cream, heavy cream, orange zest, orange juice, vanilla extract, and a pinch of salt. Beat until smooth and well combined, scraping down the sides of the bowl as needed.
   4. Pour the cheesecake filling over the cooled crust in the springform pan, smoothing it out into an even layer with a spatula.
   5. Place the cheesecake in the preheated oven and bake for 45-50 minutes, or until the edges are set and the center is slightly jiggly.
   6. Once baked, turn off the oven and let the cheesecake cool in the oven with the door slightly ajar for about 1 hour.
   7. Remove the cheesecake from the oven and let it cool completely at room temperature. Once cooled, refrigerate the cheesecake for at least 4 hours or overnight to chill and set.

3. Making the Chocolate Ganache Topping:

   1. In a small saucepan, heat the heavy cream over medium heat until it just begins to simmer.
   2. Place the sugar-free chocolate chips in a heatproof bowl. Pour the hot cream over the chocolate chips and let it sit for 1-2 minutes.
   3. Stir the chocolate and cream together until smooth and glossy, forming a ganache.

4. Assembling the Cheesecake:

   1. Remove the chilled cheesecake from the refrigerator and carefully remove it from the springform pan.
   2. Pour the chocolate ganache over the top of the cheesecake, spreading it out into an even layer with a spatula.
   3. Garnish the cheesecake with orange zest, if desired.
   4. Slice and serve your sugar-free chocolate orange cheesecake chilled. Enjoy!

This cheesecake is creamy, decadent, and bursting with the flavors of chocolate and orange, making it a perfect dessert for any special occasion!

Sugar-Free Chocolate Walnut Blondies

Ingredients:

- 1/2 cup unsalted butter, melted
- 3/4 cup powdered erythritol or your preferred sugar-free sweetener
- 2 large eggs
- 1 teaspoon vanilla extract
- 1 cup almond flour
- 1/4 cup coconut flour
- 1/4 teaspoon baking powder
- Pinch of salt
- 1/2 cup sugar-free chocolate chips
- 1/2 cup chopped walnuts

Instructions:

1. Preheat your oven to 350°F (175°C). Grease an 8x8 inch baking pan or line it with parchment paper for easy removal.
2. In a mixing bowl, combine the melted butter and powdered erythritol. Mix until well combined.
3. Add the eggs and vanilla extract to the butter mixture, and beat until smooth.
4. In a separate bowl, whisk together the almond flour, coconut flour, baking powder, and a pinch of salt.
5. Gradually add the dry ingredients to the wet ingredients, stirring until a thick batter forms.
6. Fold in the sugar-free chocolate chips and chopped walnuts until evenly distributed throughout the batter.
7. Spread the batter evenly into the prepared baking pan.
8. Bake in the preheated oven for 20-25 minutes, or until the edges are golden brown and a toothpick inserted into the center comes out with a few moist crumbs.
9. Remove the blondies from the oven and let them cool completely in the pan before slicing and serving.
10. Once cooled, slice the blondies into squares and enjoy!

These sugar-free chocolate walnut blondies are perfect for satisfying your sweet tooth without the added sugar. Enjoy them as a delicious snack or dessert!

Sugar-Free Chocolate Peanut Butter Nice Cream

Ingredients:

- 4 ripe bananas, peeled, sliced, and frozen
- 2 tablespoons unsweetened cocoa powder
- 2 tablespoons unsweetened peanut butter (or any nut or seed butter of your choice)
- 1 teaspoon vanilla extract
- Optional toppings: chopped nuts, sugar-free chocolate chips, shredded coconut

Instructions:

1. Place the frozen banana slices in a food processor or high-powered blender.
2. Add the cocoa powder, unsweetened peanut butter, and vanilla extract to the blender.
3. Blend the ingredients until smooth and creamy, scraping down the sides of the blender as needed. You may need to pause and scrape down the sides a few times to ensure everything is well mixed.
4. Once the mixture is smooth and creamy, taste and adjust the flavor as needed. You can add more cocoa powder for a richer chocolate flavor or more peanut butter for a stronger peanut butter taste.
5. If the nice cream is too soft, you can transfer it to a freezer-safe container and freeze it for 1-2 hours until it reaches your desired consistency.
6. Once the nice cream is firm enough, scoop it into bowls and serve immediately.
7. Garnish with your favorite toppings, such as chopped nuts, sugar-free chocolate chips, or shredded coconut.
8. Enjoy your sugar-free chocolate peanut butter nice cream as a refreshing and guilt-free dessert!

This nice cream is dairy-free, sugar-free, and packed with natural sweetness from the bananas. It's a perfect treat for hot summer days or anytime you're craving something sweet and satisfying.

Sugar-Free Chocolate Avocado Cookies

Ingredients:

- 1 ripe avocado, mashed (about 1/2 cup)
- 1/4 cup unsweetened applesauce
- 1/4 cup unsweetened cocoa powder
- 1/4 cup powdered erythritol or your preferred sugar-free sweetener
- 1 teaspoon vanilla extract
- 1 cup almond flour
- 1/4 teaspoon baking soda
- Pinch of salt
- 1/4 cup sugar-free chocolate chips

Instructions:

1. Preheat your oven to 350°F (175°C). Line a baking sheet with parchment paper or a silicone baking mat.
2. In a mixing bowl, combine the mashed avocado, unsweetened applesauce, unsweetened cocoa powder, powdered erythritol, and vanilla extract. Mix until well combined and smooth.
3. In a separate bowl, whisk together the almond flour, baking soda, and a pinch of salt.
4. Gradually add the dry ingredients to the wet ingredients, stirring until a thick cookie dough forms.
5. Fold in the sugar-free chocolate chips until evenly distributed throughout the dough.
6. Using a spoon or cookie scoop, drop tablespoon-sized portions of dough onto the prepared baking sheet, spacing them about 2 inches apart.
7. Gently flatten each cookie with the back of a spoon or your fingers, as they will not spread much during baking.
8. Bake in the preheated oven for 10-12 minutes, or until the cookies are set and slightly firm to the touch.
9. Remove the cookies from the oven and let them cool on the baking sheet for a few minutes before transferring them to a wire rack to cool completely.
10. Once cooled, serve your sugar-free chocolate avocado cookies and enjoy!

These cookies are a healthier alternative to traditional chocolate cookies, thanks to the avocado and applesauce, which provide moisture and natural sweetness. They're perfect for satisfying your chocolate cravings without the added sugar!

Sugar-Free Chocolate Hazelnut Granola Bars

Ingredients:

- 1 1/2 cups rolled oats
- 1/2 cup chopped hazelnuts
- 1/4 cup unsweetened shredded coconut
- 1/4 cup unsweetened cocoa powder
- 1/4 cup powdered erythritol or your preferred sugar-free sweetener
- 1/4 cup coconut oil, melted
- 1/4 cup sugar-free maple syrup or any sugar-free liquid sweetener
- 1 teaspoon vanilla extract
- Pinch of salt
- 1/4 cup sugar-free chocolate chips (optional)

Instructions:

1. Preheat your oven to 350°F (175°C). Line an 8x8 inch baking pan with parchment paper, leaving some overhang on the sides for easy removal.
2. In a large mixing bowl, combine the rolled oats, chopped hazelnuts, unsweetened shredded coconut, unsweetened cocoa powder, and powdered erythritol. Stir until well combined.
3. In a separate bowl, whisk together the melted coconut oil, sugar-free maple syrup, vanilla extract, and a pinch of salt.
4. Pour the wet ingredients over the dry ingredients and mix until everything is evenly coated.
5. If using, fold in the sugar-free chocolate chips until evenly distributed throughout the mixture.
6. Transfer the mixture to the prepared baking pan and press it down firmly into an even layer using a spatula or your hands.
7. Bake in the preheated oven for 20-25 minutes, or until the edges are golden brown and the granola bars are set.
8. Remove the pan from the oven and let the granola bars cool completely in the pan.
9. Once cooled, use the parchment paper overhang to lift the granola bars out of the pan. Place them on a cutting board and slice into bars or squares using a sharp knife.
10. Store the sugar-free chocolate hazelnut granola bars in an airtight container at room temperature for up to one week, or in the refrigerator for longer freshness.

These granola bars are packed with protein, fiber, and healthy fats, making them a perfect on-the-go snack or a quick breakfast option. Enjoy!

Sugar-Free Chocolate Raspberry Chia Popsicles

Ingredients:

- 1 cup fresh or frozen raspberries
- 2 tablespoons powdered erythritol or your preferred sugar-free sweetener
- 1 tablespoon chia seeds
- 1/2 cup unsweetened almond milk or any milk of your choice
- 1/4 cup sugar-free chocolate chips
- Popsicle molds

Instructions:

1. In a blender, combine the raspberries and powdered erythritol. Blend until smooth.
2. Transfer the raspberry mixture to a bowl and stir in the chia seeds. Let it sit for about 10-15 minutes to allow the chia seeds to absorb some of the liquid and thicken the mixture.
3. In a small saucepan, heat the unsweetened almond milk over medium heat until it just begins to simmer. Remove from heat and add the sugar-free chocolate chips to the hot milk. Let it sit for 1-2 minutes, then stir until the chocolate chips are completely melted and the mixture is smooth.
4. Allow the chocolate mixture to cool slightly.
5. Fill each popsicle mold halfway with the raspberry chia mixture.
6. Pour the cooled chocolate mixture on top of the raspberry chia mixture in each popsicle mold, filling them to the top.
7. Insert popsicle sticks into the molds and freeze for at least 4-6 hours, or until the popsicles are completely frozen.
8. Once frozen, remove the popsicles from the molds by running them under warm water for a few seconds. Gently pull on the sticks to release the popsicles.
9. Serve your sugar-free chocolate raspberry chia popsicles immediately and enjoy!

These popsicles are not only delicious but also packed with fiber, antioxidants, and healthy fats from the raspberries and chia seeds. They're a guilt-free treat that everyone will love!

www.ingramcontent.com/pod-product-compliance
Lightning Source LLC
LaVergne TN
LVHW081616060526
838201LV00054B/2274